THE
Queen's
STANDARD

A 21-DAY INTERACTIVE DEVOTIONAL FOR WOMEN

THE *Queen's* STANDARD

A 21-DAY INTERACTIVE DEVOTIONAL FOR WOMEN

KENYOTTA SANIA

KEEN VISION PUBLISHING

Printed in the United States of America
Keen Vision Publishing, LLC
www.keen-vision.com
ISBN: 978-1-948270-84-7

Dedicated to my handsome sons, Emory Blake &
Terrance Deshone. Thank you for inspiring me to be the Queen
God created me to be. I love you!

Hey Queen

First of all, understand that there is nothing regular or normal about the woman reading this book. You, my dear, are a queen. That is not just what I think about you — it is what the Father says about you. (1 Peter 2:9)

There are standards for queens that go beyond what we wear or how we wave our hand. It's about being healed and whole in every aspect of our lives. This book, *The Queen's Standard*, will help you achieve just that.

Throughout this 21 day interactive devotional, we will explore God's standards for Queens. Each day comes equipped with an encouraging word, a prayer focus, theme songs, and space to journal. We will discuss a queen's productivity, rest habits, heart posture, mindset, identity, and so much more. Again, the focus is complete healing and wholeness.

All you need for this journey is an open mind, an open heart, and a writing utensil. You can take this journey alone, or invite your favorite Queens to join you for the ride. As you experience each day, be intentional about your self-reflection and improvement. My prayer is that when the journey is over, you will have a new found love for the Queen looking back at you in the mirror.

Kenyotta Sania

Table of Contents

THE QUEEN'S STANDARD PLAYLIST

Using your phone's camera, scan the QR Code below to download The Queen's Standard Playlist on Apple Music!

Day One

QUEENS KNOW WHEN TO LET GO

"First pay attention to me and relax. Now you can take it easy you're in good hands."

Proverbs 1:33 (MSG)

Worship Song of The Day *Pour it Out by Cristabel Clack*

Motivational Song of the Day *Run the World by Beyonce*

Today is the day that you let it all go! Yes, it hurts. No, you don't have a full understanding of what happened or why. You may never know or understand, but you, my dear, must learn to be okay with that.

Be okay with the fact that things did not work the way you planned. *Be okay* with the fact that the path you set for yourself has changed. Come to a resolve that your life is not yours. You are in the hands of The Great I Am. You may have experienced pure hell for most of your life, but if you choose to relinquish all control to the Father, you will find out that there is no greater place to be than in His hands.

Today's Prayer Focus Father, forgive me for holding on to my past. I have made idols of my past regrets and grudges in my heart. I have allowed them to keep me stagnant from going forward in Your Will for my life. Father, thank you for not giving up on me or canceling my assignment while I was stagnant in purpose. On this day, I release and renounce every ungodly soul tie that has had my attention. I decree and declare that on this day, I am redeemed, set free, and delivered from the past, from hurt, shame, and depression. I am the healed of God and I will walk boldly into the next level that has been prepared for me.

Let's Journal...

Your Majesty, what do you need to release?
Journal your response below.

_____

_____

_____

_____

_____

_____

_____

_____

_____

_____

_____

_____

_____

_____

_____

_____

_____

_____

_____

_____

_____

_____

_____

_____

_____

Day Two

QUEENS SURROUND THEMSELVES WITH WISE COUNSEL

So – join the company of good men and women, keep your feet on the tried and- true paths.

Proverbs 2:20 (MSG)

Worship Song of The Day *Gracefully Broken by Tasha Cobbs*

Motivational Song of the Day *Still Standing by Monica*

W e are not called to do life alone. We were created for community. Ecclesiastes 4:9-12 (KJV) shows us why community is so important:

> *Two are better than one, because they have a good return for their labor: If either of them falls down, one can help the other up. But pity anyone who falls and has no one to help them up. Also, if two lie down together, they will keep warm. But how can one keep warm alone? Though one may be overpowered, two can defend themselves. A cord of three strands is not quickly broken.*

You may be thinking, "That sounds good, but I don't trust people!" Well, queen, it's time to start. Despite the bad experiences you may have had, God has ordained individuals to walk through life with you. Ask for His guidance in selecting people who will hold you accountable and push you to be the best queen you can be. If you allow Him to, God will send you trusted family and friends to be a safe place for you. He will send those who will walk with you through dark seasons, and celebrate you in seasons of success. From this day forward, decide not to do life alone, but in the company of godly men and women.

Today's Prayer Focus Father, deliver me from my trust issues. Heal the places in my heart that have been bruised because of let downs and heartbreaks. Help me to open my heart to trust, love, and be loved. Allow me to encounter godly men and women who have my best interest at heart. Give me godly discernment in my relationships. I declare that I will no longer isolate myself, but I am open to the relationships, wise counsel, and connections You desire to bring into my life.

Let's Journal...

Your Majesty, who's on your wise counsel? Why are you connected to these individuals? Journal your response below.

_____

_____

_____

_____

_____

_____

_____

_____

_____

_____

_____

_____

_____

_____

_____

_____

_____

_____

_____

_____

_____

_____

_____

_____

_____

_____

_____

Day Three

QUEENS HAVE A SECRET PLACE

"Here's what I want you to do: Find a quiet, secluded place so you won't be tempted to role-play before God. Just be there as simply and honestly as you can manage. The focus will shift from you to God and you will begin to sense his grace."

Matthew 6:6 (MSG)

Worship Song of The Day *Make Room by Jonathan McReynolds*

Motivational Song of the Day *Sittin' Up in my Room by Brandy*

L et me ask you something, queen. Where do you go to spend quiet, alone time with God? If you don't have a space designated, you should. A queen's secret place is a space she can sit uninterrupted before the presence of God. This can be a closet, car, office, or room. Despite what the rest of the world demands of her, a queen's secret place is her freedom zone where her only requirement is to be a daughter of God. In this space, she can completely disrobe her soul with no fear or shame. It is a place of brutal honest and complete transparency. A queen can be found in her secret place frequently, for this is where she gains the strength and direction to become the best version of herself. The most beautiful thing about a queen's secret place is that in this space, she comes to a resolve about who God has called her to be and hears instructions for her future.

If you don't have a secret place, pinpoint one soon, your majesty. Healing and developing are processes that require intentionality. Creating a space for uninterrupted time with God allows you to be intentional about the healing and development you need. Locate your secret place today, and carve out time to visit it daily. The Father is waiting on you.

Today's Prayer Focus Father, lead me to my secret place. Once I am there, allow Your presence to overtake me. Immerse me in your love and grace. I want to be fully healed by You. I want to create a relationship with You that no person can ever come between. Silence my fears that I may hear everything you have to say about me. Heal the rejection and abandonment in my heart that I may be able to trust Your word. In my secret place, take me where I need to be in you.

Let's Journal...

Your Majesty, what would you like to share with God or hear from God in your secret place? Journal your response below.

_____

_____

_____

_____

_____

_____

_____

_____

_____

_____

_____

_____

_____

_____

_____

_____

_____

_____

_____

_____

_____

_____

_____

_____

_____

Day Four

QUEENS TRUST THE PROCESS

"I know what I am doing. I have it all planned out – Plans to take care of you, not abandon you, plans to give you the future you hope for."

Jeremiah 29:11 (MSG)

Worship Song of The Day *Never Lost by All Nations Worship Assembly Atlanta*

Motivational Song of the Day *Trust by Keyshia Cole*

Yes, you are an amazing planner. You know what you want, and you are not afraid to go get it. The Father made you that way, so He understands. Nevertheless, He wants you to understand that He has a plan and purpose for your life. It was created before the foundations of this world. If you would trust His plan and His process, you will see abundance in every area of your life.

Let me ask you something. Why would you want anything other than what God has ordained for your life? His resume is flawless, and all throughout the Bible, we see proof that God's plan is always best. The process of seeing the manifestation of what God has promised doesn't always feel good, but remember: He always works all things together for the good of those who love Him. All He needs you to do is trust Him.

I get it — life can make you feel like you are on the longest roller coaster ride ever! However, you must learn to embrace every turn and loop. The quicker you embrace them, the sooner you will be back on a smooth path. If nothing else, queen, trust that God always has your best interests at heart. Take a deep breath. Relinquish your control. Do what God has instructed, and trust Him to take care of the rest. Don't forget to trust every part of His immaculate process. It will be worth it.

Today's Prayer Focus Father, it's difficult at times, but I choose to trust You. I will not lean to my own understanding. Instead, I will lean on Your Word and reputation. You promised to never leave or forsake me, and I trust you. When my mind fills with doubt remind me of Your promises to care for me and give me a hope and future. More than anything, give me the strength to embrace and endure your process.

Let's Journal...

Your Majesty, what promises are you waiting for God to fulfill?
How has the process been thus far? Journal your response below.

_____

_____

_____

_____

_____

_____

_____

_____

_____

_____

_____

_____

_____

_____

_____

_____

_____

_____

_____

_____

_____

_____

_____

_____

_____

_____

_____

_____

_____

Day Five

QUEENS TAKE TIME TO HEAL

But I will restore you to health and heal your wounds, declares the Lord.

Jeremiah 30:17 (MSG)

Worship Song of The Day *Consuming Fire by The Well*

Motivational Song of the Day *Flawless by Beyoncé*

Smile, Queen. Today is going to be a beautiful day. You have accepted the past for what it was and now you have decided to trust God on this beautiful journey. Becoming completely healed and whole takes time and intentionality. Along the way, you will have to take captive every negative thought about your process. When the enemy throws lies at you and tries to make you feel defeated on your journey to wholeness, you must discipline yourself to respond with the Truth in the Word of God.

Be careful not to compare your journey to others. Steer clear of feeling like you should be further ahead. Take a deep breath and be present right where you are. The truth is, you are not where you were last year. You've evolved and are still evolving. You've survived seasons you thought would kill you. The pain and hurt from your past made you think you would never see the light of day, but look at you! You are living, breathing, and healing.

No matter where you are in your healing process, hold your head high. Straighten your crown and smile. Be kind to yourself and remain faithful to God. Pretty soon, you will be right where you've always desired to be. Healing looks good on you, Queen.

Today's Prayer Focus Father, help me to be patient with myself as I heal. Help me to trust that You know about every broken place in my heart and are working in me to heal those places daily. I desire to be whole, and I know I can only do that with You. I cast discouragement and hopelessness out of my heart and mind. I decree and declare that I am a new creature in You. Thank You for promising to complete the process You have begun in me. Keep me in perfect peace as You fulfill every Word You've spoken over my life.

Let's Journal...

Your Majesty, what's the most frustrating part about your healing process? How will you deal with those frustrations? Journal your response below.

_____

_____

_____

_____

_____

_____

_____

_____

_____

_____

_____

_____

_____

_____

_____

_____

_____

_____

_____

_____

_____

Day Six

QUEENS TAKE TIME TO PROCESS THEIR EMOTIONS

Go ahead and be angry. You do well to be angry — but don't use your anger as fuel for revenge. And don't stay angry. Don't go to bed angry. Don't give the devil that kind of foot hold in your life.

Ephesians 4:26 (MSG)

Worship Song of The Day *Real Thing by Maverick City Music (Dante Bowe)*
Motivational Song of the Day *Level Up by Ciara*

You've been pressing through hardships, trials, let downs, tribulations, and frustration. Despite everything life has thrown your way, you have been relentless and resilient. Your strength is commendable, and I'm proud of you. But today, it is time to take a deep breath and feel every emotion you've swept under the rug.

You may not realize it, but every unprocessed emotion is slowing you down. That's right, queen. It has become baggage and weight in your soul. That is why it has felt so hard to move forward. I know you don't feel like crying and "being all emotional," but the longer you hold it in, the harder it will become to keep moving forward with life.

In order to fully process your emotions, you must be honest with yourself. Take some time to allow yourself to feel. The thing about emotions is that they eventually come out. Don't allow your emotions to catch you off guard. Take the time to process them. No one can see you but God. Allow yourself to laugh, cry, be angry, or pout. Do whatever you need to do to process the emotions you've hidden from from the world. Trust me — you will feel so much lighter after you do.

Today's Prayer Focus Father, I've been holding on to a lot, and I'm ready to release it. Guide me through processing my emotions. Help me to uncover and accept the sad moments. Give me resolve and peace about the situations that angered me. Help me also embrace the excitement and joy I have about the success I haven't celebrated because of guilt or shame. Today, teach me how to manage and process my emotions. Show me how to allow my emotions to guide me to Your feet, instead of away. Thank you for giving me emotions to express how I feel. I look forward to learning how to embrace them.

Let's Journal...

Your Majesty, what emotions have you swept under the rug?
Journal your response below.

_____

_____

_____

_____

_____

_____

_____

_____

_____

_____

_____

_____

_____

_____

_____

_____

_____

_____

_____

_____

_____

_____

_____

_____

_____

_____

_____

_____

_____

_____

Day Seven

QUEENS KNOW WHO THEY ARE

But you are the ones chosen by God, chosen for the high calling of priestly work, chosen to be a holy people, God's instruments to do his work and speak out for him, to tell others of the night- and- day difference he made for you – from nothing to something, from rejected to accepted.

1 Peter 2:9 (MSG)

Worship Song of The Day *Glory to the Lamb by Geoffrey Golden*

Motivational Song of the Day *Firework by Katy Perry*

Aqueen knows that she is not defined by titles, positions, or relationships. She understands that God created her to be much more. Her flaws don't take away from her identity, she embraces her flaws as she allows God to work in her to correct them.

Queens don't allow the difficulties of life to redefine her. Instead, she uses them as lessons and fuel to become all that God has created her to be. She understands that her light isn't dimmed by other people's lights. A queen has no problem shining besides others. Additionally, queens don't mind helping others to see their own light. She understands that the other's progress doesn't mean her regress.

Finally, a queen knows that who she is evolves each day. She embraces when God reveals something new about her, and she is excited to learn more.

Today, spend some time embracing who you are. Identify your strengths and weaknesses. Understand what you like and dislike. Ask God to reveal who He designed you to be. If there are places in you that you haven't embraced, spend some time embracing every little thing. As a queen, it is vital that you are sure and resolute in who you are. If you are unaware of who you are, that's okay. It is never too late to start the journey to find out.

Today's Prayer Focus Father, I want to be as clear as possible about who I am. Reveal to me why You saw fit to place me in the earth. Show me why you keep waking me up day after day, despite my mistakes. Remove any unhealthy attachments I may have to statuses, relationships, titles, and positions. I no longer want those roles to define me. My desire is to understand who You say I am.

Let's Journal...

Your Majesty, who are you? Journal your
response below.

_____

_____

_____

_____

_____

_____

_____

_____

_____

_____

_____

_____

_____

_____

_____

_____

_____

_____

_____

_____

_____

_____

_____

_____

Day Eight

QUEENS ALWAYS START WITH WHY

Summing it all up friends, I'd say you'll do best by filling your minds and meditating on things true, noble, reputable, authentic, compelling, gracious- the best, not the worst; the beautiful, not the ugly; things to praise, not things to curse.

Philippians 4:8 (MSG)

Worship Song of The Day *The Worship Medley by Tye Tribbett*

Motivational Song of the Day *Life is a Highway by Rascal Flatts*

Hey, Queen! What keeps you going? What is the one thing that gives you another boost of energy for your goals whenever you think about it? Is it putting your mom in a house, seeing your dad smile, making your siblings proud, or leaving a legacy for your children? What is it?

Your why is vital to your success, and you must keep it front and center at all times. When you are tired, drained, and feel like quitting, your why will keep you going. When you don't see how it's going to happen, your why will help you keep the faith. When no one seems to be supporting you, your why will push you across the finish line. Whenever you set a new goal or focus for your life, be sure to start with why you want to accomplish it.

Today's Prayer Focus Father, You do everything for a purpose. My desire is to operate in purpose as well. Help me to remember the purpose for everything You have called me to put my hands on. Show me how to align my purpose for doing everything with your will for my life. Guard me from desiring things for superficial purposes. If my why does not lead back to You, help me to redefine it. As we continue along this journey, give me the strength I need to keep pushing. If I have placed my focus and drive in the wrong place, help me shift. May I lean deeper into You to see the true plans You have for my life.

Let's Journal...

Your Majesty, in the space below, journal your goals. Beside each goal, write your why.

_____

_____

_____

_____

_____

_____

_____

_____

_____

_____

_____

_____

_____

_____

_____

_____

_____

_____

_____

_____

_____

_____

_____

_____

QUEENS DEAL WITH THE ROOT

God, my God, I yelled for help and you put me together. God, you pulled me out of the grave, gave me another chance at life when I was down and out.

Psalms 30: 2-3 (MSG)

Worship Song of The Day *Satisfy by Contagious*
Motivational Song of the Day *Glorious Day by All Nations Worship Assembly Atlanta*

Everything has an origination, including our struggles. That's right. Every battle, weakness, or shortcoming you may have didn't just appear out of thin air. Whether it be generational curses, childhood trauma, or habits you picked up from friends or your environment, everything you battle with has a root. You may not be responsible for what happened to you, but you are definitely responsible for getting to the root of it and destroying it.

It is impossible to heal without getting to the root. As a queen, it's standard that you heal and heal well. Today, I want to encourage you to spend time pinpointing the origination of your battles. Do you have control issues? Are you bad with money? Do you always pick friends who drain you more than help you? Does it seem like you can never be consistent with you goals? Explore when you first noticed your struggles. As you dig for the root within you, don't forget to take a look at the patterns in your family and environment. Once you find the root, submit it to God and submit to His process of freeing you.

Today's Prayer Focus Father, I want to be more like Christ in every area of my life. I realize that I have some areas I really need to work on in my heart, mind, attitude, and productivity. Reveal the root of the areas I struggle with. Show me where my struggles originated and show me how to address it. Allow me to forgive those who may be at fault. Allow me to forgive myself. Give me the grace, peace, and strength I need as I submit to your deliverance process. I declare that the enemies I see today, I shall never see again.

Let's Journal...

Your Majesty, in the space below, list your struggles.
Then, journal about the root for each struggle you've listed.
Feel free to revisit this journaling activity as
God gives you more revelation about your struggles.

_____

_____

_____

_____

_____

_____

_____

_____

_____

_____

_____

_____

_____

_____

_____

_____

_____

_____

_____

_____

_____

_____

Day Ten

QUEENS FORGIVE OTHERS

In prayer there is a connection between what God does and what you do. You can't get forgiveness from God, for instance, without also forgiving others. If you refuse to do your part, you cut yourself off from God's part..

Matthew 6:14 -15 (MSG)

Worship Song of The Day *Pulling Me Through by Todd Dulaney*

Motivational Song of the Day *Steady Love by India Arie*

Unforgiveness is dangerous, especially for a queen. Harboring unforgiveness can cause a queen to become ill in her body and mind. Unforgiveness blocks blessings and promotions. It can cause a queen to self-sabotage every beautiful thing God sends her way. Your majesty, you have too much to do. You don't have time for terminal illnesses, stagnation, or ruined opportunities. You must be free to travel, love, explore, learn, and become all that God has destined you to become. Today, take some intentional time ensuring that your heart is clear of all unforgiveness.

When you choose to forgive, you choose to move forward in victory. Don't waddle in self pity because of what they did. Release the offense and watch as your life begins to overflow.

Today's Prayer Focus Father, I (state your name) choose to forgive (state their name) for (state the offense). I have held them captive in my heart for far too long. I release all anger, hurt, bitterness, and resentment I have towards them. Today, I choose my freedom.

Repeat this prayer focus until you have named every person and offense you need to forgive. Take a lot of deep breaths, and pace yourself. Forgiving them may be painful right now, but holding on to grudges will destroy you in the long run. This process is worth it. Don't delay. Another level of freedom awaits you.

Let's Journal...

Your Majesty, who are you struggling to forgive? Why?
Journal your response below.

_____

_____

_____

_____

_____

_____

_____

_____

_____

_____

_____

_____

_____

_____

_____

_____

_____

_____

_____

_____

_____

_____

_____

_____

_____

_____

_____

_____

_____

_____

Day Eleven

QUEENS FORGIVE THEMSELVES

Then I let it all out; I said, "I'll make a clean breast of my failure to God." Suddenly the pressure was gone- my guilt dissolved; my sin disappeared.

Psalms 32:5 (MSG)

Worship Song of The Day *No Bondage by Jubilee Worship*

Motivational Song of the Day *Love All Over Me by Monica*

Queen, take a deep breath. The time has come, and we are going to do this together. You have forgiven everyone else. Now, it's time to take a look in the mirror and forgive her. Yes, she messed up. Yes, she made mistakes. She lived below her worth and even allowed other people to treat her less than she deserved. But, guess what? She is still worthy of forgiveness.

Understand that we've all fallen short of God's glory. At some point, we've forgotten who we were and who we belonged to. We've all been guilty of allowing the hurt of our pasts to shape our lives. You are not alone.

It's time to take your joy back. Today is the day that you will walk boldly into your destiny. Take a deep breath. Look in the mirror and forgive yourself for everything. Yes, even that. Despite everything you've done, God still has a plan and a purpose for your life. You are needed and necessary in the earth. You are amazing. You are beautiful. You are loved, and you are valued. Today, as you forgive yourself, spend some time affirming yourself. Apologize to yourself for every time you've been unkind to, said bad things about, or even doubted yourself. Afterwards, in an act of faith, take a few steps around whereever you may be. You have been released into your future. Don't you dare look back.

Today's Prayer Focus Father, I forgive me. Thank You for loving me even when I treated myself like I was worthless. Thank You for not leaving me when I allowed others to take advantage of me. Thank You for perserving my life even when I mishandled the days you placed before me. More than anything, thank You for giving me a second chance.

Let's Journal...

Your Majesty, what do you need to forgive yourself for?
Journal your response below.

_____

_____

_____

_____

_____

_____

_____

_____

_____

_____

_____

_____

_____

_____

_____

_____

_____

_____

_____

_____

_____

_____

_____

_____

_____

_____

_____

_____

Day Twelve

QUEENS KNOW WHEN TO REST

By the seventh day God had finished his work. On the seventh day he rested from all his work.

Genesis 2:2 (MSG)

Worship Song of The Day *Let Praise Rise – Nbc (Dasha Moore)*

Motivational Song of the Day *Tempo – Chris Brown*

I get it. There's so much to do, and once you factor in sleep, eating, and your basic necessities, you have less than 24 hours a day to get everything done. When our plates are full, the first thing we tend to let go of is rest. We sometimes see rest as a hindrance to productivity, however, it is vital to our ability to produce. Just think about it. When you are tired, you make a lot of small mistakes. You overlook vital pieces, and later on, may have to do everything over again. Doesn't it make sense to make sure you are well-rested before you start your day?

Today, I want to challenge you to pinpoint some time to REST. I know what you're thinking. What about my to-do list? Well, what about it? The work is not going to walk away. I promise, it will be there waiting on you once you've rested. Your purpose requires the fully rested version of you. Stop wearing yourself trying to be Super Woman, you are a queen, dear. And queens ensure they get rest. Take a deep breath today and relax. Allow your mind to drift away to a quiet place. For once in your life, just enjoy the moment. Once you've rested and cleared your mind, attack those goals head on. Just don't forget to rest when your body tells you!

Today's Prayer Focus Father, thank You for rest. Rest is a form of worship to You and I will not take for granted a moment to be in Your presence. As I rest, perfect everything concerning me in my mind, body, and soul. Release me from the guilt I feel when I am away from my work, tasks, or responsibilities. In my moments of rest, immerse me in the peace that only You can provide.

Let's Journal...

Your Majesty, how do you like to relax? Journal your response below. When you are done, select one and schedule time in your schedule to do it TODAY!

_____

_____

_____

_____

_____

_____

_____

_____

_____

_____

_____

_____

_____

_____

_____

_____

_____

_____

_____

_____

_____

_____

_____

_____

_____

_____

Day Thirteen

QUEENS EMBRACE THEIR UNIQUENESS

But you are the ones chosen by God, chosen for the high calling of priestly work, chosen to be a holy people, God's instruments to do his work and speak out for him, to tell others of the night- and- day difference he made for you – from nothing to something, from rejected to accepted.

1 Peter 2:9 (MSG)

Worship Song of The Day *You Know my Name by Tasha Cobbs Leonard*

Motivational Song of the Day *If it Isn't Love by New Edition*

I s one of your ears larger than the other? Do you snort when you laugh? Do you see things different from those around you? Are you a waterbug and cry at the drop of a dime? Are you into anime, or things that others may feel is weird? As a queen, you must understand that there is no one else on this earth quite like you. Yes, there may be some similarities, but there is ONLY ONE YOU! Since the world only gets to have one of you, make it your business to embrace every part of yourself. Love your quirks and your pickiness. Be okay with your awkwardness and goofiness. Laugh at the things you find funny, even if no one else does. Cry when something moves you, even if every other eye in the room is dry. You are a gift to this world, and we don't want a carbon copy. We want, we need, and we can handle the REAL you. Can YOU handle YOU? I sure do hope so. The world is waiting to meet her.

Today's Prayer Focus Father, today I rejoice in the unique way that you made me. I bless Your name for the works of your hands. I am Your Masterpiece. Help me to find beauty in my individuality. Show me how to value the way you made me, physically, emotionally, and mentally. Give me the strength to embrace my difference even when the world around me doesn't. Show me how to march to the beat of Your drum, and not my environment. Reveal to me how you desire to use my uniqueness for Your Glory.

Let's Journal...

Your Majesty, what's unique about you?
Journal your response below.

_____

_____

_____

_____

_____

_____

_____

_____

_____

_____

_____

_____

_____

_____

_____

_____

_____

_____

_____

_____

_____

_____

_____

_____

_____

QUEENS HAVE A PLAN

And God answered; Write this. Write what you see. Write it out in big block letters so that it can be read on the run. This vision-message is a witness pointing to what's coming. It aches for the coming-it can hardly wait! And it doesn't lie If it seems slow in coming, wait. It's on its way. It will come right on time.

Habakkuk 2: 2-3 (MSG)

Worship Song of The Day *Oceans by Hillsong UNITED*

Motivational Song of the Day *Let's Get It Started by Black Eye Peas*

What does your future look like? Where will you go? What will you accomplish? Who will you become? What's your next business venture? How will you stay free from your past struggles? How will you steward the next season of your life well? If you couldn't answer those questions, it is time for you to spend think about what's ahead for you. Partner with God, write the vision for your life, and make it plain. You have a legacy to secure and dreams to fulfill. It's time to stop hitting the snooze button, wake up to who God says you are, and go after everything He said you could have.

The questions above are a great way to start mapping out your life place. As you write out your life plan, don't forget to seek God for timing and clarity.

Today's Prayer Focus Father, what is Your plan for my life? Give me wisdom about the plans You have for me. Open my ears to hear what You have to say about my time here in the earth. I surrender my will, plans, and desires to you. As I delight myself in you, fill my heart with your perfect desires for my life. I am ready to listen.

Let's Journal...

Your Majesty, What's the plan?
Journal your response below.

_____

_____

_____

_____

_____

_____

_____

_____

_____

_____

_____

_____

_____

_____

_____

_____

_____

_____

_____

_____

_____

_____

_____

_____

_____

Day Fifteen

QUEENS FOLLOW THROUGH

Endings are better than beginnings. Sticking to it is better than standing out.

Ecclesiastes 7 1:33 (MSG)

Worship Song of The Day *To Worship You I Live – Israel Houghton*

Motivational Song of the Day *Shining – DJ Khaled*

After you understand God's plan for your life, you must do the work to see His promises manifest in your life. Don't get me wrong, there are some things God will just allow to fall in your hands. It's called favor, and you've got a lot of it, Queen. However, there are some things we must put in the work for.

You don't have time to be idle, remember, you have a legacy to secure! When things get rough and you want to throw in the towel, think about the generations that will come after you. They need you to secure the land, houses, corporations, and investments God has promised you. As you put your hands to the plow, be consistent. The legacy you leave will be predicated on the work you do today. As a queen, you must be a good steward of the resources God has granted you to work with, including your health! Keep the vision at the front of your mind and pursue it with everything in you. You've got this, Queen!

Today's Prayer Focus Father teach me how to be consistent in every area of my life. I desire to follow through with the plan You have designed for my life. Focus my mind and heart on Your will that I may not stray. Thank you for setting a path before me and giving me the boldness and confidence to walk on it daily. Help me to remember that no assignment is too big for me if I partner with you. Finally, thank you for trusting me to carry out Your will.

Let's Journal...

Your Majesty, what will you put in place to ensure that you stay focused on God's plan for your life? Journal your response below.

_____

_____

_____

_____

_____

_____

_____

_____

_____

_____

_____

_____

_____

_____

_____

_____

_____

_____

_____

_____

_____

_____

_____

_____

Day Sixteen

QUEENS ARISE EARLY

She gets up before dawn to prepare breakfast for her household.

Proverbs 31:15 (MSG)

Worship Song of The Day *Good Good Father by Chris Tomlin*

Motivational Song of the Day *Party by Beyoncé*

As we discussed in Day Twelve, sometimes, it is necessary to sleep in, take off, and enjoy time to rest. However, your majesty, this shouldn't be an every day thing! Queens arise early! Trust me, I get it. Some days, those bed covers feel like they have a tight grip on you, but you must resist the urge to press snooze. GET UP! Your legacy is not going to build itself. GET UP! Do you know how many opportunities you could be missing out on because you keep hitting snooze? When you start your day late, you show up late to chances you have to being. By the way, did I mention that being tardy anywhere is a "no-no" for queens?

Rise early. Give yourself enough time to get dressed, enjoy breakfast, and prepare for the day ahead. Sometimes, the life of a queen demands that we are the first up and the last down. If you struggle with hitting the snooze button, try putting your alarm clock across the room, and when you get up to turn it off, don't get back in bed. GET UP! Prepare your queenly attire for the day, turn on the motivational song for the day, and get moving! Your legacy depends on it!

Today's Prayer Focus Father, help me to rise early and take full advantage of the day You have laid before me. I am committed to not allowing the sun to go down before I complete the tasks You've given me for the day. Thank you for giving me life, health, and strength. Help me to manage it well each and every day.

Let's Journal...

Your Majesty, what's your morning routine?
What changes will you make to have more productive days?
Journal your response below.

_____

_____

_____

_____

_____

_____

_____

_____

_____

_____

_____

_____

_____

_____

_____

_____

_____

_____

_____

_____

_____

_____

_____

_____

Day Seventeen

QUEENS VALUE QUEENS

As iron sharpens iron, so a friend sharpens a friend.

Proverbs 27:17 (MSG)

Worship Song of The Day *People by Jonathan McReynolds*

Motivational Song of the Day *Diva – Beyoncé*

Queens stick together. We never look to degrade anyone or anything. Queens are always in search of ways to uplift and motivate others. Queens are protective of those God has placed in her life. She will go to war in prayer on behalf of her family and friends. A queen doesn't waste her time gossiping or spreading rumors. She spreads positivity and tries her best to see the good in every situation.

The greatest quality of a queen is that she is loyal. Who is a queen loyal to, you ask? She is loyal to God, and God alone. A queen is loyal to the instructions and commands of God. When times are tough, she remains faithful. When things seem impossible, she presses in even harder and expects to see the promises of God. God can trust a queen because He knows she will not drop the assignment He has given her. With the help of her Heavenly Father, she goes toe to toe with the biggest giants and highest mountains. Queens are a joy to God and everyone He places in their lives. Everyone knows, there is nothing better than having a queen in your circle!

Today's Prayer Focus Father, thank You for the queens You have intentionally placed in my life. Thank You for their lives and purposes. Thank you for connecting us at the right time and the right moment. As we continue to grow together, allow our bond to become stronger as we become wiser. Thank you for giving me queens to hold me accountable and readjust my crown whenever I need it. Strengthen us as we strive daily towards being the queens You created us to be.

Let's Journal...

Your Majesty, today, spend some time reflecting on the queens in your life. How did you connect with them? What's so special about your bond? Journal your response below.

_____

_____

_____

_____

_____

_____

_____

_____

_____

_____

_____

_____

_____

_____

_____

_____

_____

_____

_____

_____

_____

_____

_____

_____

_____

_____

_____

Day Eighteen

QUEENS DON'T WASTE TIME

She keeps an eye on everyone in her household and keeps them all busy and productive.

Proverbs 31:27 (MSG)

Worship Song of The Day *Intentional by Travis Greene*

Motivational Song of the Day *Everyday I'm Hustling by Rick Ross*

Time is a gift that should not be wasted. As queens, we know this and use our time wisely. We create schedules that allow us to get the maximum amount of productivity out of every day. We understand that schedules bring about structure, create order, and leave no foothold for chaos or idleness.

In addition to scheduling out our work tasks, we also schedule time to rest, relax, enjoy our families, and hang out with other queens. If you've been feeling a little all over the place, or as if your days aren't productive, it's time to take a look at how you spend your time. Once time is gone, we can never get it back. How we spend our time determines how we transition to God's next season for our lives. As you go throughout your day, explore how you spend every moment. If you realize that you are spending alot of time doing things that are unproductive, make the necessary adjustments. Give yourself grace and be intentional about how you spend your time moving forward.

Today's Prayer Focus Father, thank You for the precious gift of time. I am grateful for every second, minute, hour, and day you grant me. Teach me how to design my days for productivity. Show me how to craft a schedule that will allow me to get my tasks done and spend time in your presence. Thank You in advance for instructing and guiding me through how I spend each day. As I learn how to be more productive, allow the works of my hand to prosper. I give You all the praise and honor for what will come out of my committment to steward time wisely.

Let's Journal...

Your Majesty, do you have a daily schedule? How have you allowed God to design your days? Journal your response below.

_____

_____

_____

_____

_____

_____

_____

_____

_____

_____

_____

_____

_____

_____

_____

_____

_____

_____

_____

_____

_____

_____

_____

_____

Day Nineteen

QUEENS ARE HONEST

When she speaks, she has something worthwhile to say, and she always says it kindly.

Proverbs 31:26 (MSG)

Worship Song of The Day *Hallelujah – The Well*

Motivational Song of the Day *Legend – Drake*

Honesty is always the best policy. Sometimes, it can be difficult to tell the truth, especially when you know it may hurt someone that you love dearly. However, you owe it to those around you to offer your honest perspective. When telling the truth seems hard, seek God's strength and ask Him to show you the proper timing. As a queen, you have to understand that even the right thing at the wrong time can be bad. Allow God to lead and show you the right moment to share. When being honest, it's also important that you share in love. Sometimes, the way you say something makes all the difference.

As you strive to be honest in your relationship with others, don't forget to be honest with yourself. If something is hurting you, admit it. If you know you've been off your game lately, own it and do better. Committing to a lifestyle of honesty is freeing and healing to the soul. It benefits everyone involved. No matter what you find yourself faced with, resolve to always be honest and true.

Today's Prayer Focus Father, give me the strength to commit to a life of honesty and truth. As I strive to be honest with others, remind me not to lean to my own understanding, but to seek Your wisdom and plan before I open my mouth about anything. Thank You, in advance, for training my tongue to share the truth in love. Even though others may not have been so kind when sharing the truth with me, I desire to be both honest and loving with others. Use me as a vessel to bring clarity, love, healing, prosperity, and accountability in the lives of those You've entrusted to me by sharing Your truth.

Let's Journal...

Your Majesty, is there a friend or loved one you need to be honest with? What do you have to share with them? Journal your letter below, and be sure to share it with them when God allows you.

_____

_____

_____

_____

_____

_____

_____

_____

_____

_____

_____

_____

_____

_____

_____

_____

_____

_____

_____

_____

_____

_____

_____

_____

_____

Day Twenty

QUEENS KNOW WHO THEY ARE (PT2)

A good woman is hard to find, and worth far more than diamonds.

Proverbs 31:10 (MSG)

Worship Song of The Day *The Prayer by The Well*

Motivational Song of the Day *Roar by Katy Perry*

Why are we having this conversation about identity again, you ask? Because it is VITAL that you are affirmed in your identity. You see, a queen's authority is rooted in knowing who she is. Knowing your God-given identity will keep you from making the same mistakes you made in the past. When you realize that you have a Father who will never turn His back on you, everything about your life changes. Your worship will change. Your prayers will become backed with more faith. You relationship with God will go to new heights and deeper depths. Being rooted in your God-given identity also changes you outwardly. You will speak different, love yourself and others better, and be even more committed to your goals. It will even change the way you present yourself to the world around you. There is something about coming into the true acceptance of your identity in Christ that makes you unstoppable. The things of the past no longer matter or hold you stagnant. Queen, once you are sure about who you are, you become free indeed.

Today's Prayer Focus Father, thank You for giving me an identity. Thank You for revealing that identity to me and teaching me to walk in it. Thank You for staying close to me as I endured the process of learning who I am. You have healed my mind, body, and soul and given me confidence in who You say I am. I am so grateful. Every day, help me to walk in the boldness of who I am as I carry out Your will on Earth as it is in Heaven.

Let's Journal...

Your Majesty, over the last 20 days, what has God revealed to you about your identity? Journal your response below.

_____

_____

_____

_____

_____

_____

_____

_____

_____

_____

_____

_____

_____

_____

_____

_____

_____

_____

_____

_____

_____

_____

_____

_____

_____

_____

_____

_____

Day Twenty-One

QUEENS TRUST GOD

"Trust God from the bottom of your heart: don't try to figure out everything on your own. Listen for God's voice in everything you do, everywhere you go; he's the one who will keep you on track. Don't assume that you know it all. Run to God! Run from evil! Your body will glow with health, your very bones will vibrate with life! Honor God with everything you own; give him the first and the best. Your barns will burst, your wine vats will brim over. But don't, dear friend, resent God's discipline; don't sulk under his loving correction. It's the child he loves that God corrects; a father's delight is behind all this."

Proverbs 3:5 (MSG)

Worship Song of The Day *Forever by Jason Nelson*

Motivational Song of the Day *Bow Down by Beyoncé*

In all you, do remember to put God first and trust Him to lead you. He has never failed, and He never will. Despite what life may throw your way, hold on to the promises and the love of the Father. The truth is, difficult things will come, and we can't always plan for them. In those moments, we must remember that God is allowing our tribulation to work for us.

Don't stay stuck when life let's you down. Choose to cling to God's unchanging hand. Your heavenly Father loves you and is always concerned about your well-being. He has also surrounded you with queens who will keep you covered in prayer. It's time to go forth! Be Bold. Be affirmed. Be determined. Remember to trust God every step of the way!

Today's Prayer Focus Father, I have resolved to trust You. When the boat of life begins to rock, help me to keep my eyes on you. When things don't go as I planned, teach me to trust that Your plan is better. When life is getting the best of me, remind me that You want what's best for me. When I feel alone, remind me that You are always there, loving, leading, and guiding me. Thank You for choosing me to be a part of Your master plan. I am here to serve to You faithfully for the rest of my days. I accept Your grace for the journey ahead.

Let's Journal...

Your Majesty, are there areas of your life where you struggle to trust God? Journal your response below.

_____

_____

_____

_____

_____

_____

_____

_____

_____

_____

_____

_____

_____

_____

_____

_____

_____

_____

_____

_____

_____

_____

_____

_____

_____

_____

_____

_____

_____

WORDS FROM THE AUTHOR

We have come to the end of our 21-day journey, but healing is a lifetime process. You may have to revisit a few days from our conversations, but the freedom you will experience on the other side is worth it. As you continue on your pursuit of healing and wholeness, remember that it is not about being perfect, but your willingness to let go. If you desire complete healing, you must allow God into your most intimate areas. You will see that will every new level you reach requires a new you. In order to get to the new you, you have to release past hurts, traumas, defeat, and deceit. By reading this book and committing to the journaling experiences, God has already began a new work in you and He will complete it. That, my fellow queen, is a promise! Be healed. Be whole. Be free, in Jesus' name. I love you, queen!

Praying for you always,
Kenyotta Sania

STAY CONNECTED

Kenyotta Sania was born in Valley, Alabama. She is the Mother of two brilliant young men, Emory Blake Brown and Terrance DeShone Hutchinson. Kenyotta is the CEO of The Regal Eagle and The Founder of The Queen's Standard. She is on a mission to build wealth, health and discipline through biblical principles. Kenyotta's one true desire is to see people become who they were originally created to be.

Thank you for reading, The Queen's Standard. Kenyotta looks forward to connecting with you. Here are a few ways you can connect with the author and stay updated on new releases, speaking engagements, products, and more.

FACEBOOK   Kenyotta Sania
INSTAGRAM   @kenyottasania
WEBSITE   www.kenyottasania.com
EMAIL   kenyottascrim@gmail.com

www.ingramcontent.com/pod-product-compliance
Lightning Source LLC
Chambersburg PA
CBHW061046110426
42740CB00049B/2418